*My*

*Rendezvous*

*with*

*Life*

BY THE AUTHOR OF
"Why Not Try God?"

# *My Rendezvous with Life*

By
Mary Pickford

Afterword by
Dr. Anke Brouwers

NORTHERN ROAD
CULVER CITY, CALIFORNIA
2013

Copyright 1935
by Mary Pickford

Afterword copyright 2013
by Dr. Anke Brouwers

Copyright 2013
First Northern Road Edition
ISBN-13: 978-0615785776
ISBN-10: 0615785778

Edition editor, Andi Hicks
Series editor, Hugh Munro Neely

Published by
Northern Road Productions
P.O. Box 954
Culver City, California 90232-0954

find us at: northern-road.com
Cover design by Hugh Munro Neely
Book design by Andi Hicks

TO
# MY MOTHER

# FOREWORD

*When we stop to consider that all of life, as we understand it, springs from a little seed, then a progression of life beyond this present experience should not seem such a miraculous thing.*

*The development of a Sequoia tree growing two hundred and fifty feet into the air and living five thousand years is, to me, more amazing than the transition we call death.*

*And so why do we humans in this world think of our progression out of it as such a great mystery when the wise ones through the ages have assured us that the only part of us that really can be destroyed is our false and limited conception of life?*

M.P.

W*HAT are we?*
*Where are we going?*

*When separation from a loved
one comes, is it for all time?*

Once I was satisfied to label such questions mysteries. I knew I was living in a remarkable age when the world was making greater progress in thought and invention than it had in the fifty centuries preceding. But it was not until sorrow came my way and I ached for reassurance that I began to appreciate the infinite secrets that are being solved about ourselves and the universe around us.

There is no time or space, I learned. And I caught a hint of their unreality when I sat in my apartment on the thirty-sixth floor of a New York hotel and talked by wireless telephone to a friend on a ship ten days across the Pacific. He was at least seven thousand miles away. But though it was the night of a certain day where he was, and the morning of the next day where I was, his voice reached me a few seconds after he spoke.

Just now I stood at my window in Beverly Hills and watched a gray plane soar across the sky. It was the first passenger air liner, a giant amphibian, that will connect this country with Hawaii and the Orient; an air clipper that will cover in hours, distances that once took months to travel.

Man is dissolving time and space!

He is conquering the skies!

Yet, not so very long ago, he was terrified to explore even the sea because he thought he would drop off the edge at the horizon!

In this year of 1935 we chuckle over the old fellows who believed in a flat world where monsters lurked at the brink to eat them up. And we cheer for Columbus and other adventurers who sailed into the unknown only to discover new lands. But let anyone dare to speculate about the uncharted seas of the present day, the seas of this life and the next, and the average man begins to wriggle uncomfortably and mutter, "Hey, don't be morbid!" or "Why bring that up?"

All the same, I'm going to bring it up. And I'll tell you why. That same average man — the one who needs it the most — muddles through his days, the plaything of his five lying senses. He seldom wakes up to what he is, or where he is going, until someone he loves disappears across this life's horizon. Then he is shocked into consciousness. Desperate for some explanation of this separation, he casts about for an answer. In striving to understand Death, he frequently stumbles on the truth about Life and the fact that we have an indestructible self that never dies. You see, I know about the shock of parting. Two of the people I loved best in this world, my mother and my brother, Jack, have crossed this world's horizon. I have been hurled right down into the lowest pit of grief. And slowly, painfully, I have climbed back to a brighter outlook where understanding replaces sorrow.

Of course we can grimly grit our teeth and bear the black pit until we get used to it. Since there is a ladder available to help us climb to a more cheerful place, why not use it? In fact, there are many different ladders. And some of you may have found one quite different from the one I have used. But since that which I — an average, hopeful woman — have come to believe may help others who find themselves hopelessly mired in sorrow; and since it may show them how to climb out of that sorrow — in other words to gain faith in God and themselves — I am writing this book.

"If a man die, shall he live again?"

Job asked that. And so have all the others who, like those doubting mariners in the time of Columbus, wonder if we tumble out of Life and into Oblivion at the horizon. Well, there was a young carpenter of Nazareth who proved that putting off the body wasn't the end. His enemies attempted to destroy him as thoroughly as they knew how; they crucified him and pierced his side and sealed him in a stone sepulcher; yet in three days he returned to show them life could not be destroyed. And I, for one, am willing to have faith in what he proved.

"The tomb is not a blind alley; it is an open thoroughfare," is the way Victor Hugo looked at it. "It closes in the twilight to open in the dawn. My work is only beginning — is hardly above the foundation. I would gladly see it mounting forever. The thirst for the Infinite proves infinity."

What a glorious feeling of release that thought gives! It divorces us from the fear of extinction. And if we are freed of the fear of death, then we are free indeed.

"My work is only beginning."

In other words, the experiences in each particular life are just the series of related incidents that go to make up all experience. When we compare the twenty or forty or eighty years of one life span with the eternity through which each one of us as immortal souls shall live, it is only like a passing moment; one to be used as profitably and happily as possible but never considered as all there is to expect.

I wish such things had been explained to me when I was a child. Somewhere, probably from my religious instruction, a ghastly fear of death was instilled in me. That dreadful little prayer, "Now I lay me down to sleep," terrified me. "If I should die before I wake" filled me with a horror of passing away in my sleep. I had hell-fire and the pictures in Dante's *Inferno* — those dismal inky engravings — and a lot of other old-school bugaboos mixed up in my young mind. And even as a tiny girl I began to dread the time when I must lose my mother.

I loved Mama so very much; we were not only mother and daughter, but the greatest friends, who worked and laughed and played together. We always talked things over. I never told her of my fear, though many nights I sobbed myself to sleep over it. All my life, even in my happiest moments, it would stab through me like a knife. And when the time came when she finally went away, my first thought was, "It has happened. The thing that has tortured me all these years is here!"

Now that childish ignorance was all wrong. Babies shouldn't be allowed to suffer like that. If I had a little girl she would be taught from the beginning that life on this plane is a game, a thrilling adventure. And that when she and I and all the others have lived this experience just as well as we know how, there will be only more thrilling adventures lying ahead, and nothing to fear, ever.

There were times in my mother's life that were very hard — times when she suffered privation and trouble and pain. But though I once raged bitterly against the injustice of such experiences coming to her, I realize now that this was not the sum and total of her life. She has progressed; and to progress means to advance toward a better state. Her span here was only a moment in eternity — as if she had fallen asleep in her own lovely garden and dreamed that she had spent years in a dank prison only to awaken a moment later to find herself safe and secure in her own place

That isn't just a fairy tale to comfort a child. It is what the great thinkers of all times have assured us. "Death is not a journeying into an unknown land," Ruskin tells us, "it is a voyage home. We are going not to a strange country, but to our Father's house, and among our kith and kin."

You see, he didn't mind making the journey. And I don't believe anyone else does when the time actually arrives. When I was eighteen years old I was so gravely ill the doctors said I couldn't live. I knew this; and I remember when the moment came that I was slipping away, I had the most marvelous feeling of lightness and well-being and peace. I thought, "So, this is it." And I was glad.

But all of a sudden a terrible clamor disturbed me. It drew me back. And when I opened my eyes I saw that it was Mother crying and taking on at a great rate. I was very much annoyed. But I looked sweetly up at her and murmured, "God bless you, Mama, darling." Then I closed my eyes again.

Now I suppose if I had really gone ahead and made the journey, my family would have remembered me as a pious little angel whose last thought was to bless her dear ones. But the truth of the matter was, I was simply trying to trick Mother into being quiet so that I could get away without any fuss. And when my plan didn't work and she kept on sobbing, I decided that it might, after all, be wrong to go away and leave her. And so I came back and got well.

Mind you, I am not saying the separation isn't pretty terrible for the ones who are left behind. No one knows that better than I do. And yet when my mother went happily away on a trip to Europe I was perfectly satisfied to remain in

Hollywood, busy with making a new picture. Mama was on the other side of the world; but because I loved her so much she seemed nearer to me than the people I could reach out and actually touch.

After all, it is not the separation that puts us on the rack so much as it is our doubts over what may be happening to the departed one. And, besides this torturing uncertainty, there is always that demon, Self-Pity, who comes to every bereaved person and slyly robs him of his last shred of courage.

Not long after my own sorrow a friend of mine, a famous comedienne, whom I shall call Ann, lost her mother. They had been inseparable companions and her grief was terrible. A mutual friend called me on the telephone and said, "Mary, try to help her. She may listen to you because she will know you understand. Anyway, we must get her out of this, or I don't know what may happen."

When I arrived at her home I was told that she was prostrated — too crushed to see anyone. But the doctor came out of her room just then and said, "Go in, Miss Pickford. You may know what to say to her."

I entered to find her in a frightful state. And as I looked at that poor moaning huddle on the bed, I realized for the first time the folly of grief. I saw then how badly I myself had acted during my own trouble. And though I ached to put my arms around her and sympathize with her, I knew that it would only send her into worse storms of weeping.

I knew she must be startled out of her misery. And so I steeled myself to say, "Ann, can you stand a good hard smack? Because that's what I'm going to give you."

She stopped moaning; and she opened her eyes and looked up at me. And then I said, "This is one of the worst cases of self-pity I ever saw in my life! The idea of your taking on like this because your mother has gone and left you! You're spoiling her happy home going, that's what you're doing! You should be ashamed to hurt her like this!"

That surprised her. After a moment

she sat up. "Do you really believe that, Mary?" she demanded. "Do you actually believe that my mother could be happy and all right somewhere?"

I sat down beside her then, and I told her how powerful our thoughts are. And that even if her mother were not able to see us — and I was not saying she couldn't — the thoughts of grief and sorrow we were broadcasting might easily be strong enough to make her utterly miserable. Ann agreed that if her mother were starting out on an earthly journey she, Ann, wouldn't ruin her trip by constantly sending her radiograms of reproach and despair at the parting. And soon, I could see that the idea was helping my friend to get hold of herself.

Finally, I said, "Why, Ann, your mother won't be alone. Your brother is there to greet her. And many more of your family and old friends will be waiting to welcome her."

"Oh, Mary, wouldn't that be wonderful!" she said. "And maybe your mother is with her, too."

## Mary Pickford

And then Ann made the first gallant step toward conquering grief. For she smiled and said, "I'll wager the first thing your mother will say to mine is, 'Linda, you should be ashamed of yourself for not saving a fortune from Ann's earnings and leaving it in trust for her.' And I can just hear Mother saying, 'Mind your own business, Charlotte. We had a darned good time spending it!' "

Laughter is a wonderful medicine. After all, wouldn't Heaven be a sad place without a sense of humor? The moment Ann could hope, she could smile.

After that her thoughts turned from herself, and guessing that I had probably hurried there without my breakfast she insisted that I must have something to eat. Presently she decided she must stop letting her emotions literally tear her to pieces; and that she would cease from poisoning the atmosphere for the friends who had come to help her. So she got up and dressed and went about, facing her trying experience with courage.

"Do you really believe she could be

happy and all right somewhere?"

Ann's question is one we all ask. Well, do you believe in God, that tremendous force who is present every where? When we came into this world He provided gentle hands to welcome us; and when we progress into the next, we will still be in His loving care.

God wouldn't make each of us a unique personality — as distinct from each other as our finger-prints are — just to wipe us out in a few brief years. He wouldn't destroy the loving work of His hands. That horizon we label extinction is a thing we only imagine — any horizon is a place we never reach.

Why can't we think of God as a kind and wise Father who has a wonderful and loving plan worked out for each of us? Even in these topsy-turvy times when the whole world seems in such a muddle, we discover that He is Good. There has never been so much of everything for our use: great catches of fish from the sea; the earth producing huge crops; so much, in fact, that we, His children, are short-sightedly destroying His gifts instead of sharing them. Don't blame God because we don't know how to use what He has provided for us. Don't blame Him for our shameful lack of love and consideration for our brother's need. When we stop running around in circles and turn to Him for guidance, when we start thinking kindness instead of hate, He'll show us how even this economic confusion can be harmonized.

If we don't believe this, we have only to look at the mess we have gotten ourselves into by thinking greed and selfishness and wars. Those destructive thoughts are what cause depressions. And nothing else! Wars in themselves are bad enough. But aside from the murder and maiming and waste and horror let loose, it is the hatred they set vibrating through the universe that generates the greatest harm. Where do you suppose that mysterious influenza epidemic came from during the World War if it wasn't nature answering man's demand for destruction? Even isolated persons having no contact with the outside world were stricken. When nations let loose their greed and hate the whole world must suffer.

By the same token, when the people of all countries have good will toward one another the entire world will benefit. Listen to what science says about the power of thought. Every time you love or pray or hate or curse, the brain moves. That movement communicates itself to the ether all around you; the ether carries it on to the Universe; and there it waits to strike on a mind in sympathy with its ideas and to become a part of that life. Remember that the joyful news of a gold strike will set the whole country to booming! Or how the fear-thought communicates itself in a financial panic! Then can't you see how virulent thoughts of doubt and grief can be? And how important it is to keep our minds from either broadcasting or receiving such thoughts?

Everything that ever was or ever will be was originally created by thought. God thought; and a universe was set in motion!

### Mary Pickford

A universe was set to vibrating! Breathtaking, isn't it? That means, then, that everything — every thought, every word, every person, every star — everything, is a rate of vibration; that is, some form of motion. And all these various rates of vibration have two aspects, visible and invisible, one you can see and one you can't.

It's like this: everything we see in this world is an objectified thought — a thought with an overcoat on. Take a tuning fork as an example. You can see only its overcoat. But you can't see its invisible vibration, the one that is intense enough to extinguish a candle if pointed toward the flame. We know that a column of marching men must break step when crossing a bridge if their invisible vibration is not to destroy the bridge. It was the vibration of the trumpets that toppled the walls of Jericho. Caruso could sing a tone that would shatter a glass.

Our bodies are objectified thoughts; they are simply the objects we dangle in front of other people to identify ourselves.

It is as if every personality in the universe — those on this plane and on all the other planes that exist — were attending a great University. In this University are many schools of experience; and in the school of this plane, your physical body and mine are the uniforms by which we recognize each other.

Do we really have another body besides this material one we can see? Metaphysicians and religionists think so. And so do philosophers and psychologists and even scientists. But since it is a spiritual body, it has a higher vibration than the physical; so when it graduates into a higher plane, it discards our school uniform and is no longer evident to our earthly senses.

We understand this better when we consider how even earthly things can become invisible before our very eyes. I caught a glimpse of this when I was crossing the continent by aeroplane recently. I was looking out at the scenery ahead when suddenly I realized I was gazing right through the giant propellers. I knew that they were there; I had seen them when the plane was at rest; but now those enormous metal blades were whirling at such terrific speed that I could not see them!

As another example, look at the slow motion pictures and their revelation of how much the human eye misses even of the things we think we can see. They prove how much is hidden from us when they slow down motion so that we have the time to take in what is actually happening.

Not a vibration, not an atom in the universe is lost for an instant. And so Why should we suppose a personality — the most precious vibration of all — can be lost?

After all, it wasn't just a physical body that made my mother who and what she was. It was her courage and love, her tenderness, her humor and generosity and patience and understanding. The endearing and lasting part of Jack's personality was made up of his gaiety, his charm and kindness and affection. These qualities with many others were the essence, the spirit and life in my dear ones. And not only do they continue to live on this plane in memory, but as a necessary part of God's universe — and in their unique combination of qualities which make up a particular personality they go on, forever imperishable.

Life cannot be destroyed. A body is put off, but that is all that happens. That is why suicide is such a foolish business. A visible body can be discarded; but the invisible essence of it, the living personality, will only find itself faced with the same problems it has attempted to escape. It is as if a person tried to sneak into a higher grade in school without having finished the lower grade. If he hadn't learned his multiplication table, how could he expect to work an algebra problem?

We can't dodge life. And so we had better face and master it. Each of us is really immortal and perfect, right this minute — only some of us are ignorant of the fact. But we are spiraling toward an understanding of our perfection. Every one of us who is looking for the truth about life is a mental explorer. When we find out that death is only life progressing beyond our physical senses, it doesn't take long for us also to realize that, no matter where we find ourselves, we think our way into all the heaven there is and we think our way into all the hell there is — in other words, that they are states of mind and not localities.

Some mental explorers may be further along the road than others. All are not on the same road. But we are all headed for the same goal — understanding. And each of us at this present moment, no matter where he finds himself in the Universe — behind a counter, driving an engine, or dwelling in the Infinite — is the result of what he has thought through the ages.

Now, I have been poor and I've been cold and I've been hungry and heartbroken. And so I'm not just talking idly when I say that it isn't what happens to us that matters a hoot. It's the way we react to each experience, what we think about it, that counts. Do we face life with hope or despair? With fear or with faith? For there was never a problem put to any of us that hadn't an answer. And the solving will depend entirely on our true attitude of mind.

Of course, if I were unarmed and came face to face with a lion, there wouldn't be much time to start throwing up mental defenses. If I were someone who had never bothered to build courage and mastery and poise in myself, I'd probably be so utterly terrified that the lion would sense he had the better of the affair and would make short work of me.

You see he'd know I was afraid. How? Some think that animals get these impressions mentally — that we actually seem to strike out at them with our fear thoughts. Others believe that the fear thought distills a poison in the system which is exuded by the body and that an animal's sense of smell is sensitive enough to pick up the message. That is why some lion tamers rub their bodies with aromatic herbs which are said to cover up that odor of fear — otherwise known as nervousness.

But there was once a man called Daniel who didn't require such aids. He had built such faith and understanding in himself that he went into a whole den of lions — and hungry lions they were, too — but they never touched him.

Daniel simply knew he was God's highest handiwork, a Man. He knew that this confidence banished fear and gave him dominion over the fiercest beasts. And because he knew it so completely, the lions knew it. And they let him alone.

The thinking of Daniel was good. He had built it strong and true. Even the lions sensed his friendly, loving attitude toward them and responded to it. All great thinkers have made unselfed love the basis of living because man and beast must react rightly to it. When Daniel — like other men — graduated into another life, that was the part of him that marched forward. He left his earthly body behind. But his right thinking body went on.

Went on where? "From light into the splendor of glory." Those grand, hopeful words are from an ancient Hebrew writing — words that cheered me so much that you might like to know the rest of the verse. It says:

"And time shall no longer age them. For in the heights of that world shall they dwell, and they shall be like unto the angels, and be made equal to the stars. And they shall be changed into every form they desire. From beauty into loveliness, and from light — into the splendor of glory."

Nothing in this universe is ever lost. Do you realize that? Substance may and does change form; but it never ceases to exist. Water merely evaporates; the form changes; but the reality is everlasting.

Remember how, at the opening of the recent Century of Progress Exposition in Chicago, the thousands of gleaming lights were switched on by the power picked up from a beam of light that had left the star, Arcturus, more than forty years ago? I suppose that anyone on Arcturus would think that little ray of light had died because it had disappeared from his world. But far from being destroyed it had traveled through space for forty light years — with who knows what fascinating adventures en route. Then it neared our planet and was caught up by astronomers; and its energy was amplified and transmitted by them to throw the master switch at a great Exposition.

The form changes — but it never stops existing. Just think about that a minute. I have a young cousin who has just come of age. It is claimed that the human body is renewed every seven years and, if this is a fact, my cousin, at twenty-one, has already had three bodies and is beginning to build the fourth. But we don't worry about those discarded bodies; and we don't spend much time sighing for the infant he once was. We adored that baby. But if he had stayed a baby, we would be heartbroken because he had not developed normally and according to the great law of Life.

Man is a progressive spirit. And

though the divine spark was always in him, the cave man started from a pretty low state of understanding to climb to his present manhood. It is still a state that is far from perfect. Which is the best reason I can offer why God wouldn't destroy us. He is a just God. And He certainly is going to give every one of us a chance to prove the powers still latent within us.

How are we going to rouse these inactive powers? By recognizing and cultivating them. Only certain centers are now working in the average man; others are dormant. In a perfect human being all the centers will function fully and will produce perfect mental unfoldment and a perfect physical body. I believe the man called Jesus was like that. He was a perfect man, a Master who knew the power of thought. Because He knew the truth about all things, He had dominion over all things. When others spoke of death, He spoke of life. He was a pattern for us to model ourselves after. "Alone in all history He estimates the greatness of man," Emerson said of Him. "One man was true to what is in me and you. He saw that God incarnates Himself in man, and evermore goes forth anew to take possession of the world."

Do you wonder what certain centers in ourselves are not functioning fully? Well, here is an example. The history of the human race goes back many thousand years. But it is only in the last few thousand years that we have begun to perceive color. At first man knew only black and white. Then red. And finally, by slow development, he saw the primary colors and their combinations. Yet even now a large percentage of people are color blind. And there are myriads of more glorious colors all around us that even the most sensitive human eye can't detect.

Think of how many make no response to music. They are what is known as "tone-deaf." They hear sounds, of course. Yet they listen to great, inspiring symphonies without the slightest reaction. Music is a closed book to them. And so we know that certain centers in those men have not yet been aroused.

All great musical artists are striving to achieve pure tone and to elevate man's thoughts by its sheer beauty. The radio is doing much to educate young people to an appreciation and understanding of music and this may one day prove of priceless worth to mankind. Harmony is a powerful force for good.

When Mama and Jack went away one of my most agonizing thoughts was whether we should ever meet again. And if we did, would we know each other? At this moment I have no positive proof that we will. By that I mean I can't show any of my five senses this will be so. But by a higher sense, the power of Intuition, I am sure that nothing can ever cut a tie of pure unselfed love. Love is God. And so long as you love anyone, you are bound by God to that person, whether he has gone on to another life or not.

God is not cruel. He would not let us down. He would not let us build a beautiful comradeship with someone only to tear us apart forever. Sometimes there must be separations, which are necessary for our growth. In this life we face them when we send our children away to school — or when we release them to set out on their own careers.

Death is just another such separation; and one that I truly believe will end in reunion. God arranged my meeting with Mother and Jack to my satisfaction in this life. And so why shouldn't I believe He will do it as happily in the next? He has given the lower animals a sixth sense called "the homing instinct." A dog will travel hundreds of miles to find the master he loves. And so why shouldn't a man, who is the highest manifestation of God's thought, be drawn intuitively to his loved ones when they meet again on other planes? These are the things that sorrow has taught me. And now that I am acquainted with grief, I have even learned that it has its virtues. Since it is an experience we all share, it becomes one of the greatest of all human bonds, one that makes us kinder to others who suffer. You see, men misunderstand each other so often because they seldom feel the same emotions at the same time; but when they feel a similar emotion simultaneously, then and then only are they bound to understand each other.

Somewhere I have read that "Happy lives are little lives. They do not live beyond their rose-wreathed walls." And so, when sorrow drives us out of our quiet gardens into the open highway, we must accept it gallantly. For along the road to understanding we will find inspiring new scenes; and even when we are traveling through the dark valley, we shall be able to see the shining mountaintops ahead.

A message that brought me the greatest comfort in my dark hours is called "The Ship*." I do not know the name of the author. But though it has frequently been quoted, I should like to repeat it. It says:

"I am standing upon the seashore. A ship at my side spreads her white sails to the morning breeze and starts for the blue lagoon.

"She is an object of beauty and strength and I stand and watch her until, at length, she is only a ribbon of white cloud just where the sea and sky come to mingle with each other.

"Then someone at my side says, 'There! She is gone!' Gone where? Gone from my sight — that is all.

"She is just as large in mast and hull as when she left my side and just as able to bear her load of living freight to the place of destination.

"Her diminished size is in me, not in her, and just at the moment when someone at my side says, 'There! She is gone' there are other voices glad to take up the shout, 'There! She comes!'"

# AFTERWORD

*My Rendezvous With Life* is a book about death. And then again it is not. Perhaps we should state instead that *My Rendezvous with Life* is a book about the rethinking, understanding and overcoming of death and that through this exercise it ultimately becomes a celebration of life. Silent screen legend Mary Pickford wrote this book in 1935, a year after the stunning success of her book called *Why Not Try God?* in which she had described her creed of positive thinking and her views on God and spirituality. *My Rendezvous With Life* continues on this path of friendly testimonial advice but it is more ambitious in its effort to offer its readers solace and understanding in times of extreme sorrow as when faced with the loss of a loved one.

Pickford knew what she was writing about: she dedicated the book to her mother, Charlotte Smith, who had died in 1928 of breast cancer. Charlotte had been Pickford's only surviving parent, her confidante, closest friend, teacher, critic and admirer, her manager and conscience. She had been, for better and for worse, Pickford's *compagnon de route*, a loyal and stable presence amongst the loneliness that fame and fortune can bring. Pickford admits that when her mother died she was violently overtaken by what she describes in her book as "the folly of grief." The book is in part a therapeutic account of her (and a friend's) struggle to deal with emotional rupture but it is also a self-help manual for others in the same situation.

While writing the book, Pickford not only had her mother but also her brother Jack on her mind. Jack Pickford had died in 1933 in Paris from the various consequences of a life of hard living. His death was obviously too soon — he was only 37 — and occurred at a time when Pickford was facing a plethora of unpleasant realizations. Professionally her screen career was over and she was running out of other options: a short radio stint did not work out; the stage had lost its charm and required a trained voice and an acting technique Pickford had grown out of; and producing for United Artists, a perennial "problem child," was often frustrating. On top of this, she was getting older herself. Now in her early forties, Pickford was confronted with the passage of time, the first signs of decay, and the possibility of death.

Despite the obvious real biographical grief, *My Rendezvous With Life* is not a weepy book. There is room for mourning but no room to cry or despair. Describing the emotional turmoil one experiences after the death of a loved one as "a folly" may strike some readers as odd or insensitive, but Pickford has a sweeping argument to make and from her own vulnerable position of having experienced immense grief herself she does not come across as harsh. Death, she comforts, is not the absolute and infinite abyss we take it to be, but rather a passing moment, a temporary separation from our loved ones. She convinces her readers by recounting personal experience, but also turns to religious and scientific sources to build her case. As she does so she sounds reassuring, soothing and kind, and quite hard to disagree with, if only because she sounds so sweet about it.

Although Pickford had not addressed the subject of death in such a methodical and lengthy manner anywhere before, she had never eschewed the dramatization of grief, death, or (spiritual) despair in her films. She had addressed death and grief quite explicitly in *Tess of the Storm Country* (1914; 1922), *Daddy-Long-Legs* (1919), *Pollyanna* (1920), *The Love Light* (1921), and *Sparrows* (1926). Surely, the subject of death is difficult to address without implicitly suggesting a religious or spiritual model and in Pickford's rendition of faith, which was in line with much of the precepts of Christian Science (toward which she had gravitated after her divorce from her first husband,) it is not a minister but a woman (mostly Pickford herself, whose angelic looks made her the right icon for a semi-religious subtext), guided by her own interpretation of scripture, who proves the most fitting embodiment of how the spiritual should be transferred to real life. Surely, her films show no interest in any thorough evaluation of faith in a dogmatic context or in dramatizing crises or extreme expressions of faith, but Pickford had never been afraid to address and dramatize faith within the logic of the household, within domestic terms as well as in terms of feelings. Of course, since Pickford's pictures were principally forms of entertainment and bound by the exigencies of dramaturgical and narrative structures, her films would only sparingly address these big questions of life and death.

In *My Rendezvous with Life* Pickford had the opportunity to flesh out her central moral and spiritual concerns in more depth. The result is a book that is touching in its genuine desire to help others going through the difficult times and notable for its ambition to realize a greater human understanding through empathy. She writes: "You see, men misunderstand each other so often because they seldom feel the same emotions at the same time; but when they feel a similar emotion simultaneously, then and then only are they bound to understand each other." It is a sentimental solution perhaps, but in Pickford's logic and persuasive rhetoric, it rings true.

ANKE BROUWERS,<br>ANTWERP, 2013

# ABOUT THE AUTHOR

Film pioneer, businesswoman, author and philanthropist Mary Pickford (1892-1979), frequently called "America's Sweetheart," was for at least twenty years of the last century the most famous woman in the world. Though best known as a star and producer of motion pictures during the silent film era, her ideas have had a profound influence on popular culture up to today.

# ABOUT THE AFTERWARD AUTHOR

Dr. Anke Brouwers teaches film history and film theory courses at the University of Antwerp and Hogeschool Gent (Kask – School of Arts). She has written a PhD on sentimentalism in the films of Mary Pickford and Frances Marion.

She has published in Quarterly Review of Film and Video, Film International and has contributed to edited collections (e.g. Slapstick Comedy, 2009, Melodrama, 2012) and conference proceedings. Research interests include cinematic narration, film and emotion, children's cinema, silent cinema and intermediality.

# A NOTE ABOUT "THE SHIP"

The poem that Ms. Pickford uses as the culmination of her work, *My Rendezvous with Life*, has an uncertain origin. For over 100 years it has been printed, reprinted and quoted, often under different titles: *Gone from my Sight*, *What is Dying*, *A Parable of Immortality*, and others. More than once, a copy of the poem, unsigned, has been found in the possession of a recently deceased person, and friends or family have presumed it to be the work of the person in whose papers it was found. In recent times it is most often attributed to Henry Van Dyke (1852-1933), however the editor of this edition has been unable to confirm that the poem appears in any of Van Dyke's published works.

At various times the poem has also been attributed to at least half a dozen other authors including, most remarkably, Victor Hugo. The earliest publication of the poem that we have been able to locate was in a Chicago Methodist newspaper, the Northwestern Christian Advocate, where it appeared in Vol. 52, No. 28, published on July 13, 1904. At that time the poem was credited to Luther F. Beecher (1813-1903), a Methodist minister. However the fact that this publication appeared just over eight months after his death makes it possible that Reverend Beecher's surviving family, discovering these inspiring words among his effects, made the same assumption that has subsequently been made by others.

The text used in *My Rendezvous with Life* differs somewhat from the text as it is most often published. Pickford also eliminates the possibly superfluous final line: "And that is dying." Those wishing to find other versions of the text for comparison can easily find multiple sources on the internet.

THE EDITOR

www.ingramcontent.com/pod-product-compliance
Lightning Source LLC
Chambersburg PA
CBHW051718040426
42446CB00008B/943